SILENCE imbibed

JENN GUTIÉRREZ

To Abby
with gratitude
for the shared
experience.

Jenn G.
'18

ANAPHORA LITERARY PRESS-
COCHRAN, GEORGIA

ANAPHORA LITERARY PRESS
163 Lucas Rd., Apt. I-2
Cochran, GA 31014
www.anaphoraliterary.wordpress.com

Book design by Anna Faktorovich, Ph.D.

Published in 2011 by Anaphora Literary Press

Silence Imbibed
Jenn Gutierrez—1st edition.

ISBN-13: 978-1-937536-10-7
ISBN-10: 1-937536-10-6

Library of Congress Control Number: 2011942885

SILENCE IMBIBED

_____

JENN GUTIERREZ

To my husband and girls.

And with gratitude to Jane Hilberry

for her feedback and support.

ACKNOWLEDGMENTS

Some of the poems in this book first appeared in the following:

The Acentos Review
Antique Children: A Mischievious Literary Art Art Journal
Underground Voices Magazine
The Bacopa Literary Review
Verdad Magazine
Flycatcher Journal

Cover Image by Kevin Mason.

CONTENTS

CAMPING at OLEJTO WASH

We woke to rain,
a light sprinkling of rhythm
and pattern against tarp.
The cadence of the San Juan,
harnessed
with silt rising.
First there was the wind.
It blew her adrift,
like those many piles
of wood we floated past—abandoned.
Here it is a constant fight for sunlight,
a play of eddies,
and sand—red sand, the colored
mask of a forgotten cheek.
How this sense of
time and place lends itself
to a permissive halt, as though it too
is searching for the you and I
immersed so long ago.
Lost wisdom of fire
ignited the old-fashioned way,
and then there is the evening—
the way the canyon cradles the moon
and Venus stands helplessly guarding.
I feel her crying
within stone walls and taste her
seeping up through the hallows
of sediment buried.
Picturing hair the color of night,

and eyes the reflection
of rushing.
Something like my own ebony eyelash
dislodged
and falling to the earth.
Descending, I am washed free—but lost
in a kind of human hollowness

of distance fighting against
the warmth of your body
spooning my own.

AFTER READING
Your Body—

So much talk about organs
with their deceptions, lamented—

denied that natural will to praise,
the pulse, the temptations that seem

a mere reflection of autonomy.
They are prisoners of a higher will

mocked for their failures,
doing only what they were meant.

Reading your body of work
is like the feel of a clay brick
wedged into my core,
earthen, heated, molten—and heavy.

HOLDING TOGETHER
in Scalding Oil

I.

She offers empanadítas,
I swallow them down forcefully,
tasting of sweat—or,
of age itself.
That musty yeast of mother's milk
calling to me through ancient song.

II.

Christmas Eve,
In the heat of her kitchen,
I knead the dough,
as the flour clings to me,
fearing its own loss of separateness.
There is the wet, sticky-glue substance of joining—
an unarticulated family tradition.

The setting, a cave of female bodies,
with their softness,
ploughing through stories
and savoring the piñons
buried within each.

III.

They wait for my eyes to meet theirs,
following that initial swallow.
I lie. Tell them how fine it tastes
there in my mouth.
But with a lack of essential moisture,
the kind brought about by time to want, to crave,
I cannot yet taste.
My gift from your grandmother this newlywed year—
a pair of argyle socks.

IV.

She personally uncurls my fingers,
rests my hand, palm-side up,
against her padded rib cage,
and places in it, a small, round, disk—
sticky-side up.

Your wife now of many years,
She leads her diminutive hands over mine,
demonstrates that crucial next step—
the pinch and twist motion
of trapping the meat inside.
"How important," she insists,
"they don't come apart
in the scalding oil."

V.

Although the pangs of my stranger qualities
still overcome me
without warning or explanation,
this year,
as if by sudden magic,
or indulgence of the universe,
I have learned to coil the dough's edges
without flaw.

Learned that in the absence of piñon,
walnuts will do.
And that your great-grandmother
sometimes made them with cow tongue
instead of roast.
Your grandmother,
as a girl, refused to eat them.
Her mother never wasted anything.
Goat's blood collected warm
from a hanging carcass,
churned into stew.

VI.

Carried upon the sound
of your grandmother's rattled voice,
and seeing through the lenses of her faraway gaze,
I witness your great-grandfather beat her mother.
A man of drink and fornication,
he is unrelenting in his role as head of home—

She places dark glasses
over her frail mother's eyes,
now blackened like a bruised carcass,
and drags her to the courthouse.
An order of restraint issued,
she makes it impossible
for her own father to ever return.
And her mother...
never regrets it.

VII.

This holiday,
your grandmother leads me in a gift.
Wrapped in sagging skin,
rolled out in the flesh of womanhood,
tied harmoniously
with the blue veins of endurance—
every one of us there,
in that kitchen,

bears witness to the pinch and twist secret
of trapping the meat inside—

that part of the recipe
which so often
goes

     unwritten.

THE RED TEMPLE

Many such children run to us,
begging.
Plead with us
to buy their trinkets,
as we step onto our bus
outside the Nasiyan Jain.

But this girl stays with me.
Something about her—

frightens me.
The bumps on her dark skin—
on her face,
and arms.

With the kind of big almond eyes
one would expect,
and parted black hair.

Perhaps suffering
from a disease
I haven't received immunization from,

yet something yearns to hold her.
to reach down,
crouch down,
upon one knee,
pull her to me,
and soften the pain—
now branded in me.

She calls to me "*Mamí*,"
is about my youngest daughter's age,
but out here,
in this suffocating heat
as it radiates down from above,
as well as up from the street,

Out here,
in this stench
of urine and cattle dung.
Begging me
not only with her words
and her eyes,
but with the full motion of her young body—

the bobble of her head,
the Namaste pose of her delicate hands
jingling with gold and sequined bangles,
and then the way too
she transforms her fingers
from the look of sacred prayer
to the asking of food,
pantomiming the act of sustenance
against pursed lips.

What does she mean,
returning to me in dreams?
Crying blood from eyes,
vomiting it from mouth.

A BEATING ECHO

October—that month and its cold
The kind that warrants this
yearning for new warmth
until I find myself again
in the place of thoughts bygone.

Shards of red and gold
drop around us—piercing.
My daughter
offers her absolute—
"Winter is coming, Mamma."
Our eyes meet.

And then comes the tug,
to the comforts of our home, the blaze
of a wood-burning fireplace,
and the consolation that I am fully grown—
How she reaches for my soul.

Bracing against the chill,
a song of autumn plays on.
In the background, the audible swirl,
that *swish* following a playful u-turn *whoosh*,
while a heater attempts to fill space.
The silence left by
a broken stereo.

She peers out windows,
chanting words borrowed
for just such an occasion,

"Look at the mountains,
Mamma,
the sky."
I do,
And inhale.

Like a gust blowing outside in,
my husband later
holds me against the images which

dare to yank me back
To the time
when I lacked a conscience,

To the time
when I was her age,
and I failed to have the strength

to seal out that echo
of my own mother's falsetto song.

ACACIA

The air teems with frenzied bodies.
I am wandering a park located obtrusively—
smack in the middle of Downtown.
I rest on an iron bench, and soft flesh
held behind the light cloth of my gauchoed-pants,
presses through.

This is the right place,
a place which disallows firm grasping,
where flowers can only be unearthed,
not forcefully seeded
beneath so many feet. There,
on a cement block a few feet away,
a boy in jeans, which gravity also finds too unyielding,
points in my direction. I look from him to the others,
to the man who chooses to sit in shadow where the slight
drop in temperature makes it okay to bundle
when all around are bare-shaven-kneed and sleeveless.

A gooey echo of girl-pitches
bubbles above the moving forms,
and the park's rim creams
with a frothy curdle of what-ifs and what-to-comes.
How truly timeless these buddings, bloomings,
dyings and bough-breakings. If only we all knew
the hidden treasure of going limp,
that way of giving permission
for seeping through—
even while held by metal slats.

THE TEMPURATURE of CAMPUS

Here it is again, fall, with its picturesque chill.
The students huddle and move in time—
the corners of a quad transected for that second saved.
And the leaves, brilliant four-spiked reminders,
dance like it's a joke and they've been
mistakenly set free.

In here, protected behind aged glass, we withdraw to
hidden caverns.
The end of a week near, we skirt the norm
and occupy only the recesses of our own inner secrets.
The cold crackle of doors being jammed against the
frames
of all that exists in this shared space resonates stiffly.
And then too, there is the pledge of dark wood
pushing against flu season regalia.

But what's not being felt is the warmth of my flesh
residing
in time with the frozen cartilage of my unpierced ears
and the
bite of my fingers as they fight against these keys.
The vivid image of your shoulders hunched upward
and all that the language of that day held for us
as we negotiated our footing, careful not
to crush the season of our touch.
Your lips felt hard yet scalding against my own—
for me,
there was no pushing back.

Folding inward,
the temperature of this day
sends me to extremes
and the brilliance of dying color
precedes the coming coma
of a hibernating memory

BEFORE EVEN OUR EYES
Had Time to Adjust

It should trigger fireworks in the night sky—
this passage from childhood to adult.
One splash of color for the way she jumped
and squealed in the contraband sprinkler
at that hole we rented down in Bessemer—
to memorialize the way she diaper-danced bass,
seeping in from the many passing lowriders—

There ought to be an expectant blast of light
and magic competing against a full moon.
At least one skyrocket for the soiled arms
and thinning back of the green hand-me-down sofa,
to make real the left behind impressions
of her constant to-and-fro climbs.

This transition merits *Black Cat*
volume. We should feel *la vibraciones*.
Feel it, in the cores of our chest cavities—
reactions *físico*
ought resonate.

So that, when we lie down at night,
we won't smart from void this devastatingly,
fearing we missed the shower storm.

SACRILEGE

Speak to me as though in secrecy,
like wind as it stirs only the branches
of those Aspens I peer at directly.
Or like rain—
the kind that pelts scent upwards
but just in those synergetic moments
when the heat of red clay
rises to greet it.

Those rarities
in the everyday
urging us to take knee
and free ourselves of four-walled structures.

Here is my church,
my garden of the gods,
And fulfilled—that haunted compromise
between civility and the frightfully untamed.
Here is where four-legged, antler-headed, find peace,
hidden among rimmon-scales of rock,
and where one willing might be lulled
with echoes etched by Anasazi
standing barren, unprotected against
an open stone façade—

I am a fugitive of forced benches and padded kneelers.

Here, at this origin of songs inspired,
where blood once emptied,
was later cleansed by tears of those
newly anointed and unaccustomed
to such painful beauty.

Live among the holy testament
of a Majestic defined,
needing no guidebook,
no glances over the shoulder. It speaks.

Whispering lines,
it threads itself
between the
ribcaged canals
of this unrestrained member
of its congregation.

MOIST

Longings
Knitted within
Night wantings
Gracing the

Secret
Crusted
Knowledge of this innocence
     like a dawn
     unaware of her

CROTCH ROCKETS

Driving due West
toward the blue ridge monuments
of this state
fallen
against the backdrop of a
smoke gray haze

some 80 miles per hour
and I think—
I can't imagine
what it might be like
on a bike

And then you are eight again
and I recognize your Spanish eyes
hold with fear
          the revving excitement
hold on
hold tight
to that black Harley cotton shirt
Inhale sweet scented smoke of plant
I remember it hummed and rattled
between unbroken
unspent secrets of back then

Like clouds on a heat mirage day
a figure emerges out of nowhere
whisks mother away—
while father was away
hush-hush
blend it now,
vroom-vroom

There's that poem forever mingled
with page—a stain
while boyhood fantasies
imbed in your ever drowning dreams
full of ever-evil deeds
Like the machine itself
so married and seared
between the polarities
that
become you
even once
defined you

No freedom without pain
you see the scar
a red hot muffler
smoking her 18-year-old flesh
or the death of a sister's lover
and the road map etched
along his buddy's face
No freedom without pain
Reminding
Forebode

And this open highway
calls to your father's
hidden ghosts
these visions
are given
not spoken
no request has ever
been mouthed free—

No freedom without pain
so married
and yet
so scathingly

     seared.

LOST TONGUE

I wonder
what we must look like to others.

The two of us,
wading against the push of white glare
under a blaring sun, our skin in obvious
contrast.

We draw near, and the dread creeps in,
the familiar shame of no language
clutching my throat as I recognize
the woman's features.

"*Ven, ven,*" she calls to us. Motioning
excited gestures. I yearn to respond,
but again find myself only nodding.

So hurtfully unwhole, so unarmed—
but no thief can steal what
does not exist. I am simply without.

I was born brown. I was accused
of being white. I spoke the language
of schoolyards and postulated
to friends and later students—believing
there existed a right way.

I was filling.
Attempting to swath with

absorbent fluff,
the enormous hole
that hid behind my tonsils,
beneath my lungs,
the one that robs my air
each time I am greeted

with open arms,
like a child returning home,
after being away for much too long.

DAUGHTER of a
Graveyard-Shift CNA

You are too young
to understand
the gravity of such slumber.

She propels herself inside
during early morning hours
while you dream—spin
through phantom playgrounds.

Her mouth refuses the term,
"graveyard," as she is
filled with olfactory knowledge
of dying flesh, and her own body
seeks temporary distance.

It blocks out the image
of circulation going bad—
from the toes up.
Momentarily forgets the sound of breath,
staggered. Prepares itself already
for the way it will return
from a few days off to find
two others gone.

Your mother swings like a
pendulum from your youthful,
to their aging,
needs. She bathes, wipes noses—
and backsides. Yours,
then theirs.

Someday, when you
are a young woman,
you will be forgiven
all the tapping to her sleeping face.
Absolved the blood-curdling
shrieks at the sounds of her
just-about-to-doze exhales.

Your innocent crimes
will be swallowed
between draughts of steaming liquid,
carried away on the tones
of feminine laughter,
just as your own body
begins ripening,
padding unconsciously,
for its own coming,
and inevitable
assaults.

DEDICATED

I used to give credit,
so accustomed,
like breathing—
give credit to my parents
for showing me what I'm not
for placing the direction not to run
for sticking up for me bloodied
and bruised when it wasn't my fault

I used to cry fire
so alive—like destiny,
cry fire when it was time to move on
from jobs
and men
and bodily yearnings

I used to have faith
so ancient, like the Prophet,
dying
faith in morality
in a sense
       of decency
       and in

       self-discipline

PASTORAL LESSONS

The music blares from suspended speakers.
Some mornings, it is too cool to swim,
but not today—today the glare of heat
circulates the waiting mamas and papas
like halos of model parenthood.

When the instructors call time,
you see the children emerge
with their newfound pride,
shaking off the droplets
of their less-experienced selves.

Not one of them will remember
the exact sound of this place,
the way it lulls them without trying.
It is only the parents whose yearnings
will remain audible above
the noisy splash of it all.

Their love for their own offspring is apparent—
upon first glance, they are cordial
and encouraging in their common goal,
bent each of them on the molding—

But no amount of friendly exchanges
will drown the fact that they are
in the midst of racing—
racing toward that invisible tape, believing
fully in its existence, inching
their own just a little further ahead.

There are others out there,
beyond that six-foot privacy fence.
They think they have earned this station,
not that skin privilege gave them a different starting
line.
They blame the others for their own lack of ambition,
and they have their own worries, the race for instance.
Weekends during summer, they pack up
and drive to their mountain condos,
singing alphabet and number songs.

When they come to the family
holding prayer pleas at the four-way cross,
they realize their lips are chapped,
busy themselves at the bottom
of their bags, searching.

It makes for a perfect image.
They value salvation, but reject
the notion of earning it,
the gift they were born with,
a faith you hold
when you have the luxury of leisure.

I am sitting here too—
I try to focus on the music.
Try pretending the fence
is there only for the children's safety.
I alienate myself from the exchanges,
busy myself in this notebook.

When the coaches call time,
I reach down to the bottom of my own bag,
searching—

On the way out,
I deposit loose change
into the waiting hands
of the other family at the corner,
implore them to pray—
pray for my salvation.

IN YOUTH

They hoped you'd wrap yourself about the spine,
squeeze syllables from between your thighs
on Open-Call Night.
Disinterested in what it is like
to be a mother—drifting off mid-stanza,
to mentally practice their own manuscripts,
just as you came to the part about your role as wife.
Preferring the pants of your breath
against the coiled head of a mic
to your rendition of inherited family recipes.

That was not what they wiggled themselves
down into the first few rows to hear when they
first spotted your name on the yellow ledger pad
making its rounds, its lines quickly filling with
the names of tortured souls just pathetic enough
to hear themselves speak
in a room full of strangers.

Their turns up,
they'd peer out at you in ways
they would never have had the guts to do otherwise,
shielded behind that pseudonym of Art.

Once your outward features
began its task of wither,
they were more apt to listen,
but even now,
they still appreciate a good mix of nasty,
scattered auspiciously into a frisky line or two,
thinking it great fun
to hear an old woman
speak of such things.

INERTIA

Go for that walk
Maybe you will get
to watch your child
run like time
across an open field

Go for that walk
There may be
a small doe
waiting along the edge
of the gravel path

Go and hold hands
with your husband,
link arms as you once did
Stop to watch the hawk
perched in the Aspen and listen
to the panicked squawks
from those smaller

Go for that walk
Even
        if you are tired
Even
        if there are still
        dishes to be done

Go for that walk
     especially when you'd
     rather write

Go for that walk

Join them so you
can be captured too

Join them so that
the picture in their minds
will hold more
than just your silhouette

THE UNDYING TRUST
of One So Young

Death clings to our home—
Involuntary bug-animal slaughters
by innocent hands.

She yearns to learn them.
Crushes them to her understanding.
Our two black Labs her faithful minions.

First there was the garter,
slithering its need
for compassion into our hearts—
teeth marks clearly visible.

The squirrel we're unsure of,
but she found it first,
crouching low.

My mother's fear calling
down to her from the patio above—
Don't touch it!

"Its eyes are open."

The etymologist sacrifices ten
to comprehend the one.
Wings partially torn,
the June Bugs putting up
civil resistance—hunger strikes
in a cage too full of food.

Yesterday a full grown rabbit,
motionless in the front lawn.
It somehow knew, here was the place
to covet its final rest.

I envy her sense of ease,
the way she has circumvented
her parents' would-be instinct
to shield her
from life's passings.

The way she has chosen to listen
to a different calling—

And look directly upon life's offerings,
to study *Los Ojos*...
the **Eyes**.

MERGE

Because it could be—
a calling
sitting behind this desk
with designated places for neat stacks,
but comfort
embraced
in papers strewn
I find today I am
toe-fondling my own soul

Granting myself
a moment for forgetting
in the heat of natural lighting
next to an open window,
in this quietude of planning period
undisturbed
solitude treated like
a rare taste of drug
I once knew

She wears
the banner of mentor—
scraping herself against
the broken drawer of that desk belonging to
phantom rhythms of a school-house built
on the motivation of white collars

This is the jumping off point
sweet grape sugar on lips
no longer kissed
by the pulsation of pen to tip
to the fold of a nice page
too straight for leaving un-tousled or ripped

A transformation to a somebody
in a room with all eyes
in a place teeming transferred ecstasy—
the bliss of knowing you play a part
a welcome find
after all the leaps
to *Triggering Towns* on
pages too open for depth
and too shallow for contemplation

and yet,
there is still that he-she-it pandering
against the flesh of an exposed knee
to contend with

the kind that forces remembrance—
with a hint more streaming
with a little light bandaging...

the merging is not entirely out of reach

OFFERINGS

Today, I hand him gifts unwrapped:
The walking stick unadorned,
Sanded only to reveal
its natural knots and curvature.

He calls me apologetic—
Tells me he is sorry he fell asleep
and didn't say goodbye.

He adds feathers,
pilfered from
a previous gift.
Still, he is unspeaking—
But like a great crested flycatcher,
come to reclaim herself in
the cavity of all this fragmented
language,
she will spread her shadow,
circling my father's worn body.
He'll squint up to her,
from this place still rooted by gravity,
but held now upright
by the aid of a daughter's gift.

And he'll call to her
with a silence that
will always
scream too loudly
for a child's heart
to bear.

THE COLOR OF FOREIGN AFFAIRS

I.

Under the heavy sorrow
of thick-shadowed blues and
unintelligible grays,
I struggle,

See their faces
in the dimpled features of my daughter,
feel, rather than hear,
an inward screaming
from regions of my own body
too dark to mention

Somewhere
there is an infant being torn inside out.
A doctor
will later attempt
to rejoin her flesh
in the colorless voids
that will never be overcome,
and a nurse's stained hands
will bear the weight
of instruments she'll wish
were wands

Stitching closure to
another pained day,
if driven by nothing more than

pure impulse,
my body in front of this keyboard,

    is saying something

II.

That their pleas cannot go quite believed
from a modern regime sealed off—
ubiquitous. That in this age,
a power of one can still deceive

in a tone all pervasive, ominous,
the famine masses of a whole nation.
And that we, preferring instead
to dismiss tales, "preposterous"

can sit back,
imply patience.
All this and more I mourn.
I am no longer consoled
with ideas of penance,

the nullification of
"To each his own once dead."
There exists a litany of history.
Horrors that came true,
after unveiled mysteries

of crimes unheard of,
lay before us then new.
Our grandfathers and
grandmothers held ears
to radio reports that
drew blush yet chilled their flesh
to ashen hues.

In the wake
of repeated bellows
that resound with an echo
of tortures not unheard of,
in this legacy of,
"reap what one sows,"

children are beaten, torn,
and sold by once-women, once-men.
Leaving them to their own fate,
we contend—
there's just no way to be sure
action will be deemed justified.

III.

Far from the security of this soft bed,
there is a child's small limb
falling away from its North motherland.
Ancestors of a cease fire hold its hopeless
form to the chest of one about to put it on market.
It will sell for the highest bidding and fill
the craving cavity of another mother's son.

We call this humanity.

REMEMBERING

It's not difficult
to visualize them with their
flowing flaxen hair.

Not hard to picture their
pretty red petticoats flapping
in time to their skips.

And it's not too terribly daunting a task
to see just how steadily they
roam on the hind-quartered
halves of horses steered by
handsome young Harry's,
Heathcliffe's or Harvey's.

Ken was an ingenious substitute
for our cravings tempered
by our crestfallen hopes
of being rescued.

My biggest mistake ever was in forgetting.
I know that at one time I knew such secrets.

Once upon a starry moonlit night,
I was well-equipped to discern the faces
of archetypal evil dressed in the garb of heroes
or unassuming comforts.

A race of literary women wrote them into poems
and essays—even laid them out nakedly between
the pages of fiction. And I read them, understood
them,
took them to pen.

"The irreversibility of time
constitutes an objective moral criterion,"
calls Adorno. He must have done it too once—
forgotten that is. Later remembering, he wrote
it down for us again. Buried deep within the
complex phrasing, it is there waiting.
He wrote of the way in which Time herself
demands implicit exclusiveness, as who we
are at any one moment in time and who we meet when,
creates an experience unduplicated. And it is in this
genuine nature that we cling.

At the instance one body's path
through this life entangles
with another, there is no going back.

Fear of never being able to again recreate
that instance in Time, we hold tight to the one
phenomenal body who shared it with us,
objectifying the individual
whom we sought only to love.
The minute we turn that someone
into an object of our affection, that someone
transforms into a thing
and we possessors.

There is an unnatural desire in being possessed.
False words of denial fall from our lips, but
our bodies yearn to have someone fight for us—
fight over us—cut open nasty old wolves for us.

It is written in the chronicles of all ancient
text—
Boy meets girl.
Boy and girl fall in love.
You know the rest, but don't you see?
Time is the culprit—
boy can forsake girl—swallow her whole,
but he can never...

    unmeet her.

SERVICE LEARNING

Her name is Martha, and her nose
is all but worn away. As if death
has started before her, as though
she missed the cue for letting go.
Today she is less distant, but only
for one—

I try relieving the young
girl, but Martha turns on me.
Her skeletal hand reaches
up and pulls the child back down
while the other continues stroking
the fabric penguin they have made together.
We know she has something to tell us,
but it doesn't make its way out
into the air encircling the three of us,
and yet it binds with a kind of
muffled force.

Martha finds something there,
something that has triggered her
into this moment of grasping,
longing for words not entirely
forgotten.

And when it is time to leave,
I notice she has two penguins now.
Someone—
has mastered the craft of hearing.

SOCIAL SUICIDE
for my tortured students

The girl shies away from social decorum
then wraps unwanted arms around them
when they are not looking.
A child, she speaks out when no one else
is listening and shelters thoughts
that could earn her respect.

She is too far from anything I know
and too hard to keep hold of.
She is searching, and I know my place.
It is not in helping.
She is justice unwritten and water uncontained.
She will become the woman eating at the table next to
us,
the one with the book and a curtain of hair behind
which
the eyes of forced sainthood peer out tentatively
cautiously,
longingly.
If you happen to make contact,
she will recoil her gaze.
She will shift her weight and draw her back straight,
turn her head sidewise, telling you
she doesn't care
does not want
does not bleed
can no longer feel.
She is in your classes,

riding your subway car,
following behind you at the market.
And we leave her there uninterrupted
undisturbed
unknown—
undone
unsheathed,
pulled flesh off bone in a society

that prefers decorum
over
compassion.

YOU NAME IT

Each of us carries the infinite burden
of impossibilities,
a list of all we cannot
one day choose to do.

Determinism is a haze,
a firm truth that defies
clear definitions.

I cannot be an architect—
and you cannot crawl into
the cockpit of a DA20 Katana.

The longing for could-have-been's
too easily rise to the surface.
That stamp of potentialities
which brands itself into us at birth,
and the cruelest act is its stripping—
like the many layers of dead skin
we peel from our bodies
at every wash, or like
the moving images of the
digital slideshow we frame,
transitioning one past image of
what-if's to the next.

We must take stock, though,
inventory all fulfillment.
Think of them instead like
pages turning in this one
we chose to remove from the shelf.

Doing so, the story of a family
emerges like a beacon,
calling us back to

the fledgling binding
of shared thoughts and dreams.

INTIMATE
Readers

You have
surrendered yourself
full-binded.
Offered these lines
for their scrutiny,
and ask for their
molesting strokes
of good company,
as they turn you.
Allude seldom,
Skip metaphor almost entirely.
Permit emotion—
even a whole stanza,
of political angst.
But most of all,
permit their forefingers
to trace you,
to fondle you,
      at their own
      inner margins.

DELIBERATE INDIFFERENCE

This daughter's daughter
has grandmothers
and great-grandmothers
still washing dishes,
preparing meals,
pouring hot metal pots
of green chile with crippling,
arthritic fingers,
wound about ladles,
Mexican clay casserole dishes—
yielding stories through intoxicated lips

This daughter's daughter
is entering the shared existence
of this, our gender's calling,
and all her mother can do
is shrug.

CONFLUENCE

That place where two come to flow as one
It was the quench of thirst that drove us
along the ridge of cliffs,

Against the pain of our arches,
reaching for a knowing,
the throb in our heads telling us we're
still on trail

Where else in life can you mark
your way by the assurance of
cairns?

My waters push against your own,
but this murkiness?
Still an achievement.

A R T vs. L I F E

We are not so different
from our fathers and mothers.

Where they drove by houses
they couldn't afford,
we hoard manuscripts
of one-time friends,
only half-heartedly hoping
to one day haul them out
and say, "I knew him when."

Where our mothers dragged us
to ballet and ice skating classes,
dressed us in bows and silk ties,
we cram our own children's bedrooms
with shelves full of titles
we wish someone had known enough
to tell us to read.

Sometimes, we turn to Buddha,
try recalling the wisdom
behind letting go of all want—
but even then,

we cannot help wondering
if this dictum of his faith,
was not the doing of some
unnamed woman
in his ancient life.

And so we continue
to label and compartmentalize
our mirage of larger than life,
close our eyes tight,
to bury them in pillows
and dizzying familiar scents
of mortal hair and aging flesh—
lull ourselves off
to distant lands
with the phantasmal pantomime,
and our voices poised ready.

WET

A tale that speaks of treading,
treading so long, one's limbs go numb

A head can detach like a floating orbit
    rolling over waves, not crashing

There is no swallowing the enormity
    of this nothingness

And the perching of a single creature
    is just that—a perching

An Art for teetering,
    a resolve for resting.

BIRD HUNTING

This single act of innocence
and the sobering knowledge
of death.

See the chocolate wisps of hair about her face.
Notice the old milk jugs newly filled
just beyond that sidewalk
linking farm porch to Summer Home.

She is twelve now—old enough, if she practices.
She is a girl—gendered unfairly,
if we think about it.

They are all inside,
unaware of what will happen next,
unprepared for the wake
of this youthful brutality.

Watch as she shoots upward,
aiming intentionally.
The soft warm body folds itself
involuntarily against
the bare of her hands,
as she lifts it from its cradle of earth.
So fragile, this life.
She is faced with darkness bread
from her own inner terrors.

She doesn't know why she's done it.
She'll run now to where they are gathered.
Unaffected, the eldest will grab it by the legs,
ram its feathered head
against the nearest plaster of wall.
The sound ominous.
It lives on.
In her.
That thud of once-mortal.

BEHIND TINTED WINDOWS

She leans over
to the passenger side,
glancing down at her lap,
stealing glimpses into the
rear-view mirror, even though,
there is no one else
behind her.

A kindred spirit,
I imagine her into life,
curls pushed from her face
in irritated fashion
each time she arises
from her frantic search—
a scrap of paper, perhaps
the blank side of a deposit slip—
and a pen.

I think maybe
there is a soft-covered book
in her hands, peeled back and
propped against the steering wheel.
Needing to look busy, so
the other moms
will understand why
she chooses not to join them
on the well-manicured patch of lawn,
beneath the low limbs of tree
protecting the cobble-stoned path,
once donated by a well-meaning heiress.

For just this sliver of instant,
in the wake of my child's private-school,
privileged life,
I imagine spaces
reserved for us, me and my
imaginary kindred spirit,
there squeezed between the SUV's
and Mercedes.

We are safe here,
along the small strip of public curb
which surrounds our alien-children's lives.

CAPTURING HER FLAG

In the linoleum—
in the home on Walnut Drive,
little faces appearing magically
in each four inch square and drawn covertly
into the stems and buds
of the flowered shower curtain.
There—an eye or two.
The floor register was in on it too—
and in retaliation, she'd blind it
with unsuspecting, freshly-laundered
bath towels.

Mother would come in after her,
shout at finding another one wasted,
She'd smile at her little triumph,
hidden safely beneath the covers of her bed,
already quite dry.

Years spent waging these battles,
against images of little old men and women, witches,
goblins and ghouls who had no other choice
but to surrender. She emerged victorious
into the span of adolescence.

In the shadow of their tombs,
She basks in the glory-ritual of
applying her first lines of beauty paint.

And when the long awaited time
has arrived for her to pick up a razor,
the true sign of a girl's coming-of-age,
she has no trouble pushing aside their remains
to drape her leg over the tub and find a better angle.

Feels little remorse at lifting the one-time
blindfold to swipe it along the arch of distance
between wet ankle and calf—

And gives even littler thought at stepping on
their once looming profiles as she crosses
the length of their sacred trails—
on her way to a somewhat
less-memorable
first date.

DAGGERS

Without thinking,
from the back corner
of the cupboard shelf
reserved for things
no longer used—

Tired, slammed unsuspecting
by yet another migraine,
I muse a while about how happy
this ceramic vessel might be over my mistake.
Sitting there day after day,
watching me grab the others
off the space below, those
still in active duty.
Wondering about my ability
to ignore one so obviously adorned
with the symbolism of affection.

I can hear the shocked chorus
of arrogant porcelains,
belittled suddenly by the callousness
of my betrayal. Feel the daggers
of their looming mortality hit center,
just as moments ago,
preoccupied with the throb
of rebellious brain tissue,
I had pondered my own.

RELICS

Papas, the word for potatoes,
on the tongue of a one-year-old,
it becomes the universal call for all food.
At the bonk of a head, the stub of a toe,
she holds petite body parts to your lips
for the remedy of kiss to a fresh wound,
crying *"lla-lla."* And by the coming nightfall,
rubbing eyes, pretend snoring,
she follows it by yawning *"mi-mis,"*
to signal her emergent bi-lingual sleep.

Their presence in our lives,
a beacon to the voice our parents
and grandparents abandoned,
thinking they'd give us the shield
their own parents were left too unarmed to give.
Each of them coveting the language
buried within, recalling twelve-inch rulers
to the back of the hands, delivered mostly by nuns.

Disallowed the acknowledgement in school,
by mid-adolescent evenings, they could no longer
vocalize to their parents how hard it was
living amongst this discord of sound.
We honor them now with these tiny
two-syllable tributes to their sacrifice.

THE ART of STEALING

In our living room this evening
I give-in to a daughter's pleas:
"Draw with me?"

I flip through the learn-to-draw pages,
envisioning my own strokes—
an imitation, but not really.
My mind travels to the story I am
reading, the way the author
describes artists who use imitation
as a source of inspiration—
and the way a camera telepathically
captures more of the photographer
than his subjects.

I settle on a woman. Her hair spiked
in all directions, her lower lip
a shade lighter than the top.
With colored pencils,
I make her look collaged. A broken image
that when held at arms length will come alive.
Acutely aware of these fragments,
I temper them with careful detail.
Bold lines in this direction, then
that. Hints of purple behind her eyes,
highlighted in her hair
and the brown skin tones
of her exposed shoulders.

Glancing over at my daughter's picture, I try thinking
of my father and the way this craft was handed down,
the way I once admired his painted horses in motion.
How he sometimes erased my lines
to give those remaining clearer direction.
I imagine someone finding these little collections
signed "Mommy," and piecing together some analysis
of their unintended meanings. Wonder if
that someone will hold at arm's length
this idea of fragments and imitation.

SHARING YOUR BED

I.

The way an infant will
survey your face close up—
not just your eyes,
but scan the forehead,
cheeks and chin,
the space
where jaw meets ear, with equally
unabashed interest.

II.

When she comes back to
searching your eyes,
there is a way about it
that stretches somewhere far beyond
the two of you in that bed.

III.

He'll poke randomly at your lashes.
Force you to blind, despite his size,
stick an already-been-chewed index finger
into the unsuspecting caverns
of your nostrils.

V.

She'll never cease to find funny,
the propping of her feet up to your nose
for you to feign reaction,
"pee-yew!"

VI.

Most of all,
you love the way
a little one can be overcome
by the sudden need to cover your lips
with his own,
grabbing onto the whole of your head,
a surprising strength,
and accompany the motion with matching,

already learned sound-effect,
"smack."

VII.

How you revel
in the sweet smell
of emerging toddler breath on her,
even as the tinge of sour
begins its transitioning assault.

VIII.

And you truly marvel at the way
this simple act of moving your body
a tad more to one side
can reward you
with this stage
of innocent intimacy.

SINGLE DADS

They stand out of place
at the corner of the women's lingerie department,
as blushing girls grab what's necessary,
barely caring to look what size.

You spot them in front of ovens,
reading the backs of boxes in the lit rooms
of their homes, through their uncurtained windows,
as you drive by in early evening.

They are the early descendants to a race of new men,
the ones we will all look back on and wonder
that we didn't notice them sooner, knowing
they must have been there all along—
comrades thrown into this silent war
of immeasurable proportions.

THE BEST GIFTS

Are those you can savor but not describe—
Surrealism brought to life,
we traveled the five hours to get there.

In the dead of winter,
single digit readings.

We donned swim trunks and bikini,
jumped in the outdoor pool.

Never having been a fan of cold,
I couldn't have pictured it.

The two of us, floating in the
high-mineral hot springs.

Mist obstructing our view, then clearing
just enough to make out the shape of a half moon.

Allowing our limbs to gravitate
toward one another, they bumped against the discrete.

Becoming alone under a night sky, the forms
of bodies around us were made into steaming appari-
tions.

Christmas lights and music adding to
the kind of mystic ambiance, my body emanated.

Beyond the ceramic edge of boundary, thrusting heav-
enward,
I became a phantom of Time herself.

I tried looking down at this vision of male vs. female in
our material forms, but saw only the blur of flesh
against flesh.

Rich skin tones and patches of darkness,
little distinction being discerned.

And that is why when we emerged dripping and warm
from the meeting of natural wetness at her core, smell-
ing

of the mineral content of her composition, we had no
reply
for those who asked what you gave me this year.

GREEN WITH SPICE

You bring my enchilada casserole with you today,
having boyishly asked me to make it
    The *Beaners* are getting together to celebrate
I'm proud to have them taste what you have
and wish they had it too, but then I think to ask how
you will warm it, and I don't like knowing
    Rachel will warm it in her oven for you
I don't know a Rachel
You haven't mentioned her before

GROWN UP

Down a side road,
lies a no-kill shelter.
The look of grown up horror on her face
has not yet faded from memory.
The way the gentleman there
reached out to her, pleaded on her behalf,
"Do you—really have to do this?"
Guilt, the most devastating emotion.
The air here is too dry.

THE CHILDREN'S MOTHERS
of St. Jude's

Until you have relieved yourself with her on your lap,
    squiggled back into your pants one-handed

Until you have steered a cart full of groceries with one
    wrist,
    your back in the precarious shape of a violin

Until you have felt the warmth of vomit slide down
    your arm,
    and managed to not let go

Until you have had your work-clothes shot
    unexpectedly with a squirt
    of unmentionable just as your are about to head
    out the door

Until you have fought the urge to cup your hand over
    his mouth
    when he is in the midst of an exceptionally high-
    pitched scream

Until you have relinquished a portion of your bath
    water to her,
    only to have her float unwelcome intrusion into
    your midst

Only until you have kissed his closed eyelids, run a fin
    ger over his sleeping lips

or nuzzled against the soft nape of his neck as he
	drifts along
in a cloud of dreams you are too grownup to
	reach

Until you have done all this, you cannot possibly
	imagine.

What it must be like to peer down on her hospital bed,
	thinking you'd give over your own mortality
	gladly—
	if she would just get well

THE RUSE

We are all incredibly neurotic. There is a
sort of cult to reading. We know the artifacts
we accumulate to adorn our lives, and even more
crucial, the ways in which we do so, mere
expressions of the character sketches others might
form.
We could drive ourselves mad thinking about what
the order—or disorder our offices might reveal.
But that's not the secret—there is a trick.

Offer your students, readers, or whomever,
a communal self-analysis. Reveal that, when you know
someone
is coming to your home for the first time, you obsess
over your bookcases—
hiding the pulp in the back of the two column, side-
ways-packed shelves.
Showcase your favorite conversation pieces at
eye-level—
oh, and hide too, those that have been in the collection
for
more than ten years but have yet to be read beyond
their first pages.

Invite them to travel through those first tender
chapters
of our shared existence that have hitherto
and irrationally walled us up behind over-burdened
oak and maple-stained shelving.

Don't be afraid to engage perusers—
challenge them to sketch you
in a way you have yet to sketch yourself.

BODY TOLLS

In the short duration of our lives—
each no less significant for its time,
there are the global atrocities
and local brawls. Then too, there are
the many secret battles only we are privy to.

In a world where our children
grow amongst the phrases of
contemporary conflicts—phrases like
Weapons of Mass Destruction,
Suicide Bombers, Terrorists Acts,
and Biological Warfare—
we cannot fathom how the collective
subconscious of our youth might wage
horrors yet unspeakable.

In the years of our old age,
the way in which these demons
buried within the cob-webbed corners
of childhood imagination might
one day spring forth
to greet our pleas for forgiveness
in the telling of body tolls.

Using the words of Christian Crusaders
long dead, to justify our need
to "Hunt them down and kill them."
Survivors of our rubble,
will be less ready to
lie their own children in coffins,
even if the battle cry—
a herald to die for one's country,
has still yet to fade.

NO MAS

It settles itself there, in my intestines,
joins with the waste of youthful ambitions.
this knowledge that I am all at once
incapable of mourning the absence of things.
It fills me with a new layer of fortitude.

It churns in the lower organic regions,
grinds itself into a paste that will
counteract all the built up acid.

It will take care of this reflex
to spring the bile of desires unfulfilled
upward into my throat
and fling itself
at strangers unaware.

TIME THOUHGHT SACRED

Forget the lights—they are a danger anyhow.
Remember the time before dawn when strange
gurgles of sacrilege-whisperings bubbled out
of us. I will write to you of new beginnings, if you'll
only
just pause long enough. That tingle of quantum
realities where the
blue shirt you wear today is green, and where my eyes
absorb the auburn that is a reflection of my burning
nature.

We sat in a park and you mentioned them. It almost
scared you.
I told you how I dreamed of Christ walking through an
arched hall
with beams and shadows, but I don't remember walls.
We don't speak. But there is a feeling of running
towards
something. Following the path of white on cold stone
tiles,
through burdens and under curved archways. Back.
Back to dreams.
Back to make believe. Back to the mystery—
     Where things are expected, anticipated—
     to change.

OTHER ANAPHORA LITERARY PRESS TITLES

Evidence and Judgment
By Lynn Clarke

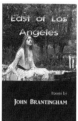

East of Los Angeles
By John Brantingham

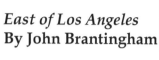

Death Is Not the Worst Thing
By T. Anders Carson

The Seventh Messenger
By Carol Costa

Rain, Rain, Go Away...
By Mary Ann Hutchison

Truths of the Heart
By G. L. Rockey

Interviews with BFF Winners
By Anna Faktorovich, Ph.D.

Compartments
By Carol Smallwood

Made in the USA
Charleston, SC
29 March 2012